THE MODERN CORPORATE HANDBOOK

— How to —
Professionally
— Say —

F*ck Off

An HR-Approved
Corporate Translation Guide
for the Professionally Exhausted

SWEET HARMONY PRESS

© 2025 Sweet Harmony Press

All rights reserved. No part of this publication may be reproduced, stored in a retrieval system, stored in a database and / or published in any form or by any means, electronic, mechanical, photocopying, recording or otherwise, without the prior written permission of the publisher.

For bulk sales or expressions of undying gratitude contact us at info@sweetharmonypress.com

ISBN: 978-1-948713-49-8

Join our email list to be the first to learn about new releases by scanning this code:

www.sweetharmonypress.com

This book is intended purely for entertainment and humorous purposes.

The author(s) assume no responsibility for:
- Promotions gained through masterful passive-aggression
- Office allies won through strategic email precision
- Any meetings that suddenly go silent after you use one of these responses

Remember:
- Use these translations with extreme discretion
- Consider your organizational culture and context
- Maintain awareness of your company's HR policies
- Think carefully about your career objectives
- Read the room (and your employee handbook)

Professional communication should always prioritize clarity, respect, and constructive dialogue. While these translations may provide cathartic relief and humorous insight into workplace dynamics, they should be viewed as entertainment rather than a communication strategy guide.

Note: Any resemblance to actual workplace situations is purely coincidental and honestly not our problem.

INTRODUCTION

Welcome to the art of professional survival.

If you're reading this book, you've likely experienced at least one of the following:
- ❖ Sat in a meeting that should have been an email
- ❖ Received an email that should have been a conversation
- ❖ Been asked to "circle back" on something you've already explained five times
- ❖ Watched someone take credit for your work while maintaining direct eye contact
- ❖ Been told to "think outside the box" by someone who installed the box, enforces the box, and actively punishes those who leave the box

In other words, you work in an office.

The modern workplace is a fascinating ecosystem where we're expected to collaborate with people who test our last nerve, remain professional with individuals who clearly got their jobs from a cereal box, and maintain enthusiasm for "corporate culture" while watching our suggestions get ignored and then presented three months later as someone else's "innovative idea."

This guide was born from the collective sighs of office workers everywhere – those moments when what you want to say would get you fired, but what you need to say has to maintain the delicate veneer of professionalism that keeps the corporate world spinning on its axis of forced politeness.

Within these pages, you'll find carefully crafted translations for every workplace scenario that makes you wish your laptop camera could convey eye rolls. From dealing with that one coworker who keeps "forgetting" to do their part of the project, to responding to the seventh unnecessary reply-all email of the day, we've got you covered with responses that are just professional enough to avoid a visit from HR.

Remember, in a world where "per my last email" is considered a declaration of war, and "as previously discussed" carries more shade than an eclipse, your choice of words matters. This guide will help you navigate the fine line between professional communication and letting everyone know exactly what you think – all while maintaining your job security.

Consider this book your Rosetta Stone for corporate communication, translating what you wish you could say into what you should probably say instead. Use it wisely, use it well, and remember – the best revenge is a perfectly worded email with your boss cc'd.

Welcome to the art of saying "f*ck off" so professionally that you might get promoted for it.

*Note: The author bears no responsibility for any promotions, office alliances, or perfectly executed email takedowns that may result from the use of this guide.

How to Use This Guide

1. Find your scenario
2. Read both versions
3. Take a deep breath
4. Use the professional version
5. Keep the other version in your heart where it belongs

Now, let's learn to translate your workplace rage into corporate-approved communication...

When you really want to say:

F*ck off.

Professional alternative:

I'll be sure to give this request the attention it deserves.

When you really want to say:

This is complete bullsh*t.

Professional alternative:

I have some significant concerns about the validity of this approach.

When you really want to say:

I don't give a sh*t.

Professional alternative:

I'll defer to the team's expertise on this matter.

When you really want to say:

Are you f*cking kidding me?

Professional alternative:

I find myself questioning the underlying assumptions here.

When you really want to say:

What the actual f*ck?

Professional alternative:

This requires further clarification to ensure alignment with our objectives.

When you really want to say:

Read the damn email.

Professional alternative:

As previously communicated in extensive detail...

When you really want to say:

Get your sh*t together.

Professional alternative:

In the interest of operational efficiency...

When you really want to say:

Stop sending me this crap.

Professional alternative:

To optimize our communication workflow...

When you really want to say:

For f*ck's sake, check your calendar.

Professional alternative:

As noted in the original calendar invitation...

When you really want to say:

Who the hell approved this?

Professional alternative:

I'm interested in understanding the approval process that was followed.

When you really want to say:

This meeting is a waste of my f*cking time.

Professional alternative:

I believe my time might be better allocated to other priorities.

When you really want to say:

I don't give a rat's *ss about your PowerPoint.

Professional alternative:

Perhaps we could focus on actionable outcomes.

When you really want to say:

Holy sh*t, this is so stupid.

Professional alternative:

I have some alternative perspectives to consider.

When you really want to say:

Can you shut the f*ck up?

Professional alternative:

Let's ensure everyone has an opportunity to contribute.

When you really want to say:

Stop talking out of your *ss.

Professional alternative:

Could you share the data supporting that conclusion?

When you really want to say:

I'm not doing this sh*t.

Professional alternative:

This falls outside the scope of our agreed deliverables.

When you really want to say:

Fix your own damn problems.

Professional alternative:

This presents an opportunity for autonomous problem-solving.

When you really want to say:

This project is f*cked.

Professional alternative:

Current metrics suggest we should reevaluate our approach.

When you really want to say:

Who screwed this up?

Professional alternative:

Let's conduct a thorough process review.

When you really want to say:

Not my f*cking problem.

Professional alternative:

This falls under another department's purview.

When you really want to say:

Pay your damn invoice.

Professional alternative:

We appreciate your attention to pending payment matters.

When you really want to say:

Stop being an *sshole.

Professional alternative:

Let's maintain professional discourse moving forward.

When you really want to say:

Do your own f*cking work.

Professional alternative:

This presents an excellent opportunity for independent development.

When you really want to say:

That's a load of bullsh*t.

Professional alternative:

There appears to be a misalignment between our understandings.

When you really want to say:

I don't get paid enough for this sh*t.

Professional alternative:

This exceeds the scope of our current arrangement.

When you really want to say:

Stop kissing *ss.

Professional alternative:

Your enthusiasm for leadership alignment is noted.

When you really want to say:

Do some f*cking work for once.

Professional alternative:

I look forward to your direct contributions to this initiative.

When you really want to say:

This is a clusterf*ck.

Professional alternative:

The current situation requires immediate strategic reorganization.

When you really want to say:

I'm surrounded by f*cking idiots.

Professional alternative:

Our team might benefit from additional professional development opportunities.

When you really want to say:

Your sh*tty attitude is toxic.

Professional alternative:

Your current approach may be impacting team dynamics.

When you really want to say:

Take this feedback and shove it.

Professional alternative:

I appreciate your perspective and will give it appropriate consideration.

When you really want to say:

Your metrics are bullsh*t.

Professional alternative:

These performance indicators may not fully capture the scope of my contributions.

When you really want to say:

Write me up, I don't give a f*ck.

Professional alternative:

I acknowledge receipt of your concerns and reserve the right to provide a formal response.

When you really want to say:

This review is a damn joke.

Professional alternative:

I believe there may be some gaps in the evaluation process.

When you really want to say:

Go f*ck yourself and your goals.

Professional alternative:

I'd like to discuss alternative approaches to measuring success.

When you really want to say:

Fix your sh*tty internet.

Professional alternative:

Your current connectivity issues are impacting our collaboration efficiency.

When you really want to say:

Mute your damn microphone.

Professional alternative:

There seems to be some background audio affecting our call quality.

When you really want to say:

Stop f*cking messaging me all day.

Professional alternative:

Let's establish some communication protocols to maximize productivity.

When you really want to say:

This conference call is bullsh*t.

Professional alternative:

Perhaps this discussion would be more effective via asynchronous channels.

When you really want to say:

How about changing out of your f*cking pajamas?

Professional alternative:

Let's ensure we're maintaining appropriate professional presentation standards.

When you really want to say:

This company culture is f*cked.

Professional alternative:

There may be opportunities to enhance our organizational dynamics.

When you really want to say:

What dumbass wrote this policy?

Professional alternative:

I have some suggestions for policy optimization.

When you really want to say:

This training is a waste of f*cking time.

Professional alternative:

I question the ROI of this professional development initiative.

When you really want to say:

Keep your damn pizza party.

Professional alternative:

Alternative forms of recognition might better serve team morale.

When you really want to say:

Your 'open door policy' is a complete joke.

Professional alternative:

The current feedback channels may need refinement.

When you really want to say:

The CEO is full of sh*t.

Professional alternative:

There appears to be a disconnect between executive vision and operational realities.

When you really want to say:

F*ck your corporate values.

Professional alternative:

I suggest we revisit how our stated principles align with current practices.

When you really want to say:

This restructuring is horsesh*t.

Professional alternative:

The organizational changes may benefit from additional stakeholder input.

When you really want to say:

Your mission statement is a f*cking fairytale.

Professional alternative:

Our operational practices might need realignment with our stated objectives.

When you really want to say:

Who's *ss did you kiss to get here?

Professional alternative:

Your career progression path is certainly noteworthy.

When you really want to say:

Pay your f*cking bill first.

Professional alternative:

We look forward to proceeding once the current invoice has been processed.

When you really want to say:

Read the damn contract.

Professional alternative:

I'll direct your attention to section 3.2 of our service agreement.

When you really want to say:

Stop being such a cheap *ss.

Professional alternative:

Our pricing reflects industry-standard value metrics.

When you really want to say:

Your idea is f*cking stupid.

Professional alternative:

Let me propose an alternative approach based on market research.

When you really want to say:

Do you think I'm your b*tch?

Professional alternative:

This request falls outside our established scope of services.

When you really want to say:

I'm not your damn personal assistant.

Professional alternative:

For efficient service delivery, please direct requests through our established channels.

When you really want to say:

Stop changing your sh*t last minute.

Professional alternative:

Late-stage revisions may impact project timelines and deliverables.

When you really want to say:

Your feedback is bullsh*t.

Professional alternative:

Your suggestions present some interesting logistical considerations.

When you really want to say:

Fix your own damn problems.

Professional alternative:

This situation presents an opportunity for internal resolution.

When you really want to say:

Who the f*ck approved this client?

Professional alternative:

The current client relationship structure may warrant review.

When you really want to say:

This paperwork is bullsh*t.

Professional alternative:

Our administrative processes may benefit from streamlining.

When you really want to say:

Sign the damn form already.

Professional alternative:

Pending approvals are impacting project critical paths.

When you really want to say:

What f*cking department does this?

Professional alternative:

I'm seeking clarification on departmental ownership of this process.

When you really want to say:

This approval chain is f*cked.

Professional alternative:

Our current approval workflow may be creating operational inefficiencies.

When you really want to say:

I'm not filling out another damn form.

Professional alternative:

This may present an opportunity to consolidate documentation requirements.

When you really want to say:

Who's the *sshole blocking this?

Professional alternative:

Could you help me identify the current approval bottleneck?

When you really want to say:

This process is like a dog chasing it's f*cking tail.

Professional alternative:

The current workflow appears to have redundant approval stages.

When you really want to say:

Cut the red tape bullsh*t.

Professional alternative:

I propose we evaluate process optimization opportunities.

When you really want to say:

Stop cc'ing the whole damn company.

Professional alternative:

Let's review our communication distribution protocols.

When you really want to say:

This compliance sh*t is ridiculous.

Professional alternative:

These requirements may warrant a cost-benefit analysis.

When you really want to say:

F*ck your processes.

Professional alternative:

Let's align our respective protocols to enhance efficiency.

When you really want to say:

This is a sh*tshow from both sides.

Professional alternative:

Current procedures are creating multiple operational challenges.

When you really want to say:

Everyone needs to get their sh*t together.

Professional alternative:

A comprehensive process review may benefit all stakeholders.

When you really want to say:

Stop wasting everyone's damn time.

Professional alternative:

Resource allocation efficiency should be our priority.

When you really want to say:

Take your policy and stick it.

Professional alternative:

Perhaps we could explore more agile implementation strategies.

When you really want to say:

Your product is sh*t.

Professional alternative:

Your solution may not fully align with our quality expectations.

When you really want to say:

Stop spamming me, for f*ck's sake.

Professional alternative:

We'll reach out when your services align with our needs.

When you really want to say:

Fix your damn delivery times.

Professional alternative:

Your current fulfillment metrics are impacting our operations.

When you really want to say:

Your support is f*cking useless.

Professional alternative:

We require enhanced technical assistance capabilities.

When you really want to say:

Who's the idiot who designed this?

Professional alternative:

The current design architecture presents unexpected challenges.

When you really want to say:

You can keep your sh*tty corporate culture.

Professional alternative:

Cultural integration requires thoughtful consideration.

When you really want to say:

F*ck your synergy.

Professional alternative:

The proposed operational alignments may need reassessment.

When you really want to say:

This merger is a clusterf*ck.

Professional alternative:

The integration process reveals opportunities for optimization.

When you really want to say:

Stop making changes in my damn department.

Professional alternative:

Our unit's current operational model warrants preservation.

When you really want to say:

Are you seriously considering f*cking layoffs?

Professional alternative:

Position consolidation will severely impact operational effectiveness.

When you really want to say:

Where the f*ck is my budget?

Professional alternative:

Seeking clarity on resource allocation timelines.

When you really want to say:

This is penny-pinching bullsh*t.

Professional alternative:

These cost constraints may impact deliverable quality.

When you really want to say:

Who's the cheap *ss who cut this?

Professional alternative:

The recent budget adjustments require strategic discussion.

When you really want to say:

I'm not doing sh*t without funding.

Professional alternative:

Project initiation awaits appropriate resource allocation.

When you really want to say:

Your ROI expectations are f*cked.

Professional alternative:

The projected returns may benefit from recalibration.

When you really want to say:

This software is complete sh*t.

Professional alternative:

The current system presents significant operational challenges.

When you really want to say:

Who f*cked up the database?

Professional alternative:

A data integrity review appears warranted.

When you really want to say:

Fix your damn servers.

Professional alternative:

System stability requires immediate attention.

When you really want to say:

This upgrade is bullsh*t.

Professional alternative:

The system enhancement may need user requirement review.

When you really want to say:

I'm not learning another f*cking platform.

Professional alternative:

Additional technology adoption impacts productivity timelines.

When you really want to say:

This strategy is pulled out of your *ss.

Professional alternative:

The proposed direction may benefit from additional market validation.

When you really want to say:

Your five-year plan is f*cking delusional.

Professional alternative:

These projections warrant careful scrutiny.

When you really want to say:

Stop moving the damn goalposts.

Professional alternative:

Objective stability ensures optimal resource allocation.

When you really want to say:

This brainstorming is bullsh*t.

Professional alternative:

Perhaps we could focus on actionable initiatives.

When you really want to say:

Take your KPIs and shove them.

Professional alternative:

Alternative success metrics may better reflect actual value creation.

Licensed Cover art:
 ID 204208022 | Angry Office Discussion © Zdenek Sasek | Dreamstime.com
 ID 287623986 | misunderstandings-team-nervous-office-workers-arguing-teamwork-communication-problems-anxiety-vector-angry-unhappy © Applikbeats777 | Dreamstime.com

www.ingramcontent.com/pod-product-compliance
Lightning Source LLC
Chambersburg PA
CBHW061810070526
44586CB00024B/2784